Leadership vs Management

Bill Vincent

Published by RWG Publishing, 2021.

While every precaution has been taken in the preparation of this book, the publisher assumes no responsibility for errors or omissions, or for damages resulting from the use of the information contained herein.

LEADERSHIP VS MANAGEMENT

First edition. August 2, 2021.

Also by Bill Vincent

Global Warning: Prophetic Details Revealed
Overcoming Obstacles
Spiritual Leadership: Kingdom Foundation Principles
Millions of Churches: Why Is the World Going to Hell?
Deep Hunger: God Will Change Your Appetite Toward Him
Defeating the Demonic Realm
Glory: Increasing God's Presence: Discover New Waves of God's Glory
Healing After Divorce: Grace, Mercy and Remarriage
Love is Waiting
Deception and Consequences Revealed: You Shall Know the Truth and the Truth Shall Set You Free
Overcoming the Power of Lust
Cover Up and Save Yourself: Revealing Sexy is Not Sexy
Heaven's Court System: Bringing Justice for All
The Angry Fighter's Story: Harness the Fire Within
The Wrestler: The Pursuit of a Dream
Beginning the Courts of Heaven: Understanding the Basics
Breaking Curses: Legal Rights in the Courts of Heaven
Writing and Publishing a Book: Secrets of a Christian Author
How to Write a Book: Step by Step Guide
The Anointing: Fresh Oil of God's Presence
Spiritual Leadership: Kingdom Foundation Principles Second Edition
The Courts of Heaven: How to Present Your Case
The Jezebel Spirit: Tactics of Jezebel's Control
Heaven's Angels: The Nature and Ranking of Angels
Don't Know What to Do?: Discover Promotion in the Wilderness
Word of the Lord: Prophetic Word for 2020
The Coronavirus Prophecy

Increase Your Anointing: Discover the Supernatural
Apostolic Breakthrough: Birthing God's Purposes
The Healing Power of God: Releasing the Power of the Holy
Spirit
The Secret Place of God's Power: Revelations of God's Word
The Rapture: Details of the Second Coming of Christ
Increase of Revelation and Restoration: Reveal, Recover &
Restore
Leadership vs Management
Restoration of the Soul: The Presence of God Changes
Everything

Watch for more at https://revivalwavesofgloryministries.com/.

Leadership vs Management

John Maxwell once said a director says go, however a pioneer says, how about we go, and somebody once joked, When I converse with chiefs I get the inclination that they are significant when I converse with pioneers, I get the inclination that I am significant. The connection among administration and the executives has been bantered about for quite a long time. A significant number of us have had supervisors who were extraordinary administrators from a useful perspective, however not incredible pioneers. On the other side, the world has seen numerous incredible, rousing, visionary pioneers who had next to no genuine administration ability. Ostensibly, the best chief or director would be one who has the two credits. However, how would we develop these qualities in ourselves? How would we adjust and keep up with the abilities and systems of the board alongside the more profound characteristics and qualities of authority? In this course, we will show you how to do precisely that.

More than 70% of organizations say they're encountering an initiative hole. 58% of directors report they never got any administration preparing, 71% of laborers say their administrators need basic initiative abilities like designation, using time productively and group building. What's more, what's to come isn't looking a lot more brilliant. 63% of recent college grads say their authority abilities have not been adequately evolved. These measurements show that administration is an inexorably significant region that organizations should zero in on. Our course will comprise of a progression of basic conversation focuses, these are intended to cover this wide theme as altogether as conceivable to support development in these indispensable regions and to work with a genuine and productive conversation inside your association about how you can each enhance this fundamental trademark, both at work and in your own lives overall. A portion of these will be quite protracted and some will be moderately direct and brief. At the finish of this guide comes the main last advance.

Conversation time, don't skirt this, this is the main piece of this preparation, when you finish this course, you need to go through something like an hour or thereabouts going over the inquiries we supply toward the end collectively. Whoever's the big cheese in the gathering should assign a Facilitator whose Responsibility it is that each question is covered and that everybody, time allowing, can express their opinion. Ensure all commitments are esteemed, all ideas considered and all sentiments regarded.

So how about we move into the principal conversation point. Who are pioneers? There's no job in the organization that simply says pioneer. Precisely, a pioneer is an individual who exemplifies certain attributes or characteristics. There's somebody who impacts individuals to follow them. Pioneers get change going. They are in charge of the association, so they ought to have a reasonable vision and accordingly provide guidance that follows from that vision. To a degree, pioneers are likewise supervisors, since they should have superior workers ready, yet mostly pioneers are the main impetus that spikes the association ahead. Pioneers normally have devotees, yet they can likewise have subordinates, obviously, heads of an association have adherents just as subordinates since they additionally work as chiefs. Pioneers have a specific degree of allure and they appeal to individuals so that they are constrained to follow the pioneer, regardless of whether what they're strolling into is a possibly dangerous circumstance. It follows that pioneers are centered around and great at managing individuals, however simultaneously they avoid their devotees. Pioneers look for hazard, however, in reasonable sums. They face impediments and issues that might wind up serving the organization's objectives instead of obstructing it.

Pioneers might even defy norms to see their objectives accomplished. Here are a few characteristics that pioneers have. Has vision. Can focus on the vision. Inventive. Adaptable. Persuasive and inspirational. Positive and eager. Dependable. Reliable. Open. Objective situated shows others how its done. Legit and has respectability. Develops a group of capable faculty. Sets exclusive requirements and furthermore accomplishes them. Can suitably designate errands. Fit for giving genuine input and isn't apprehensive about testing the set up request of things. Who are chiefs? Chiefs essentially handle activities or things like undertakings, financial plans and courses of events and individuals, for instance, their group and their customers. The work of a director is to keep everything in line. They get things done right or potentially as upper administration directs. Directors order subordinates, their power is vested in them by the organization, and consequently the administrator guarantees that their position is utilized as proposed. Directors instruct their kin and the subordinates do it for a prize, which is in all likelihood their compensation. Directors themselves are subordinate to upper administration, and all things considered, they, as well, are paid. Directors center around work and their center is imparted to their colleagues. Directors will in general stay away from dangers and struggle at whatever point conceivable. They carry out whatever systems are required to arrive at the objectives set by the executives, who are the pioneers? Administrators complete things. Here several abilities that a supervisor can't be without. Has vision and can finish it. Moving and inspirational fit for coordinating others. Coordinated, informative. Has relational abilities. Coaches their staff. Fit for taking care of techniques, equipped for preparing, can suitably assign errands and is an essential scholar and issue solver. One rather than the other. To additional our comprehension of the two ideas of Leadership and the board, Here's additional on how unique they are from each other.

Initiative is making positive, extraordinary change, it includes making a technique that will guide the way toward that change. Individuals ought to be enabled to get the association's vision going, despite the fact that obstructions are in their way and pioneers should enable those individuals. Administration, in this way, makes a group of inspired individuals who can push the organization ahead. The board, then again, manages controlling things or potentially individuals, administrators keep everything coordinated, they direct and lead their staff in a manner that adheres to the guidelines set by the organization. There's a framework set up and supervisors may likewise utilize devices to guarantee their numbers don't drop. So supervisors plan and arrange, pioneers rouse and stir energy. Authority implies driving a gathering in a quest for a foreordained Goal. Pioneers share their vision to Others, then, at that point move and persuade individuals to conquer hindrances on the way to that vision. The board implies directing the befuddled, inspiring the unmotivated and coordinating the aimless toward a settled upon normally comparative objective.

All day every day. Initiative requires a specific range of abilities, which we'd effectively examined before, conversely, directors oversee, they don't lead. Overseeing simply includes arranging, estimating, controlling, chipping away at the financial plan, designating errands and assessing them. Chiefs allocate work to their staff, assess work and yields, counsel their colleagues about execution issues and recruit and discharge staff individuals, the director realizes what to do and gives orders, no one inquiries it. The obligations of the chief. Here are a few things chiefs are answerable for. One, arranging projects just as strategic activities. Two, executing said projects. Three, critical thinking. Four, arranging work force or hierarchical exercises or obligations. Five, making itemized financial plans. Six, making execution reports and assessing them. Seven, enrollment. Eight, inspiring and empowering others. Nine, checking whether their staff act morally. Ten, fostering their colleagues abilities and progress, both Personally and expertly. Eleven, upholding the association's principles and guidelines. Twelve, training colleagues. 13, working on the usefulness and effectiveness of their staff and friends cycles, and 14, appointing errands to preparing their colleagues.

The obligations of the pioneer. Here are a few things pioneers are liable for. One, contriving dreams and points which give guidance for the staff. Two, setting up focuses for the association like monetary targets, and so forth. Three, expecting issues. Four, Visualizing possible circumstances, Opportunities outcomes and results and such. Five, figuring out what things should be assessed and provided details regarding. Six, making new arrangements. Seven, making rules, especially those identifying with discipline. Eight, devising new jobs inside the association. Nine, settling on new gatherings or chains of command inside the association. Ten, deciding good direction of the organization's work force. Eleven, empowering individuals around them. Twelve, fostering their colleagues, bunches inside the organization and, obviously, the association. 13, arranging progression, just as getting sorted out it a short time later, and 14, all administration duties which are recorded un the past area, however they are generally assigned to others, particularly those which advance inspiration and the improvement of their staff. Which one's the more significant of the two? Presently you might be feeling that authority and the executives are totally unique, their jobs and their activities rely upon each other. They're both key to the organization's turn of events. Neither one of the ones is more prevalent than the other. Together, they guarantee that the organization works agreeably. Pioneers and administrators are diverse concerning the manner in which they persuade their staff, and this sets up the way where they follow up on their power. So in case there aren't any pioneers, there's no new course wherein to take the organization, it'll deteriorate in a matter of seconds. Furthermore, assuming there aren't any administrators, there's no design or power to protect request inside the association. Administration or the board in being what they will be, they supplement each other and permit an organization to work appropriately. Assuming you need to be effective, you should be a proficient pioneer just as an intense supervisor, particularly in case you're the owner, CEO or leader of your association. One individual can't run an organization alone. You need faculty ready and you need to convince individuals to be your ally, in your group.

Without a group, you can't seek after the bigger objectives you try to achieve. Numerous administrators totally handle their undertakings. They typically aren't pretty much as invigorating as the best chief we've talked about, yet they take care of business and that is what's significant. Nonetheless, having pioneers is additionally staggeringly significant, pioneers motivate change, they're presumably not as careful as a supervisor, however they prod their kin towards a shared objective, and that is essential to the association. No compelling reason to pick sides. One, does it should be 100% pioneer or 100% administrator all the ideal opportunity for as long as they can remember, you can adjust it and utilize the others strategies as the circumstance requires. Apply your initiative abilities in case you're certain you have a group of individuals who know their jobs and what they're intended to do. Furthermore, they ought to likewise know what the organization's objectives are, they'll network well with the pioneer as they definitely know the drill. With them you can really focus to make innovative crazy Ideas. Then again, you must be the chief when your kin are new to the work or don't have a strong handle of what they're intended to do. An administrator should direct their colleagues well, see how they're doing concerning their yields just as how they're taking care of themselves. Remember about your most significant asset, your kin. Everyone's unique and they're not robots by the same token. There's no standard catch to push for everybody to begin working or work harder or quit working, regardless of whethe chief or pioneer, they have their own particular manners o getting their kin to do what they need to complete. Individual should be overseen just as persuaded. However, when you consider the board, we don't consider managing individuals passionate prosperity. The board is task based, results arranged however that causes everything to feel excessively automated excessively confined from passionate association. In case worker aren't by and by put resources into the organization's target or their Leaders or even each other, they'll become withdrawn and unmotivated over the long haul. Pioneers and supervisor need to consider this when managing their staff, they need compassion and trust to lead their groups. What's more, thus their groups will be persuaded to turn out more enthusiastically for their chiefs.

Stuck in a full breath and express your genuine thoughts Thoughts are a two way road. The group must have more than one wellspring of thoughts. Let another person talk, let another person share their insight, let another person try out a thought Who can say for sure? It could very well be the ideal one to address the current issue. However, be cautioned that there can be obstructions to this, and that is an absence of trust. Your representatives can peruse the room, and on the off chance that they don't feel that their commitments will be useful to the group or even maneuvered carefully, they'll retain their info What's more, you'll be one conceivably notable thought short. In case there's an issue with trust in the gathering, you, the pioneer need to sort out the motivation behind why this is so and wiped out. Presently to the workers. At times you simply need to take a full breath and mention to your chief what's at the forefront of your thoughts. Obviously, when you're in an organization climate, you're typically of the outlook that in case you're not a higher up, you need to quiet down, however there will be times where you can't sit around and watch others change things for you. You need to air things out, bring up defects that individuals probably won't have seen or that individuals are too hesitant to even consider discussing. You don't generally need to be tranquil and you don't need to add like clockwork, you can begin by shouting out once in a while. You're an individual and you have the right to have your feelings heard. That is the way chiefs are made, all things considered, so don't be reluctant to pose inquiries or suggest an activity.

Peer inside yourself to draw out the genuine pioneer inside. On the off chance that you seek to turn into a pioneer, you need exclusive requirements, and that implies making a dream for yourself. What do you need? Who would you like to be? What would you like to achieve? This vision will drive you advances in quest for your objectives. Think about the accompanying inquiries. Is it true that you are an excellent worker? You should buckle down, not just that, you'll need to work more astute, to be dynamic, be interested, be prepared to hop as high as your administrator or pioneer inquires as to whether the circumstance requires it hop somewhat higher than that just in case.

Is it accurate to say that you are surpassing the measuring sticks your supervisor has given you additionally make your outcomes prominent? It'll settle on sure your supervisors must choose the option to recognize you for your diligent effort. When you become a forerunner by your own doing, you've actually had the opportunity to work similarly as hard as individuals you're instructing. Concerning individuals you encircle yourself with, would they say they are pioneer material or they devoted to the organization and advancing its turn of events? You must become acquainted with a greater amount of such individuals in your association. These individuals will uphold you and offer you guidance over the long haul. Are you equipped for placing in the work to accomplish your targets and are you resolved to do as such throughout a specific timeframe. Be focused, you'll be in this for the long stretch, so wrap up.

Furthermore, presently it's conversation time, the main piece of this preparation. Whoever's the big boss in the gathering should assign a facilitator whose duty it is that every one of the inquiries you see on your screen is covered and that everybody, time allowing, can give their opinion. Ensure all commitments are esteemed, all ideas considered and all assessments regarded.

Don't miss out!

Visit the website below and you can sign up to receive emails whenever Bill Vincent publishes a new book. There's no charge and no obligation.

https://books2read.com/r/B-A-XHBC-SVXQB

BOOKS 2 READ

Connecting independent readers to independent writers.

Also by Bill Vincent

Global Warning: Prophetic Details Revealed
Overcoming Obstacles
Spiritual Leadership: Kingdom Foundation Principles
Millions of Churches: Why Is the World Going to Hell?
Deep Hunger: God Will Change Your Appetite Toward Him
Defeating the Demonic Realm
Glory: Increasing God's Presence: Discover New Waves of God's Glory
Healing After Divorce: Grace, Mercy and Remarriage
Love is Waiting
Deception and Consequences Revealed: You Shall Know the Truth and the Truth Shall Set You Free
Overcoming the Power of Lust
Cover Up and Save Yourself: Revealing Sexy is Not Sexy
Heaven's Court System: Bringing Justice for All
The Angry Fighter's Story: Harness the Fire Within
The Wrestler: The Pursuit of a Dream
Beginning the Courts of Heaven: Understanding the Basics
Breaking Curses: Legal Rights in the Courts of Heaven
Writing and Publishing a Book: Secrets of a Christian Author
How to Write a Book: Step by Step Guide
The Anointing: Fresh Oil of God's Presence
Spiritual Leadership: Kingdom Foundation Principles Second Edition
The Courts of Heaven: How to Present Your Case
The Jezebel Spirit: Tactics of Jezebel's Control
Heaven's Angels: The Nature and Ranking of Angels
Don't Know What to Do?: Discover Promotion in the Wilderness
Word of the Lord: Prophetic Word for 2020
The Coronavirus Prophecy

Increase Your Anointing: Discover the Supernatural

Apostolic Breakthrough: Birthing God's Purposes

The Healing Power of God: Releasing the Power of the Holy Spirit

The Secret Place of God's Power: Revelations of God's Word

The Rapture: Details of the Second Coming of Christ

Increase of Revelation and Restoration: Reveal, Recover & Restore

Leadership vs Management

Restoration of the Soul: The Presence of God Changes Everything

Watch for more at https://revivalwavesofgloryministries.com/.

About the Publisher

Accepting manuscripts in the most categories. We love to help people get their words available to the world.

Revival Waves of Glory focus is to provide more options to be published. We do traditional paperbacks, hardcovers, audio books and ebooks all over the world. A traditional royalty-based publisher that offers self-publishing options, Revival Waves provides a very author friendly and transparent publishing process, with President Bill Vincent involved in the full process of your book. Send us your manuscript and we will contact you as soon as possible.

Contact: Bill Vincent at rwgpublishing@yahoo.com www.rwgpublishing.com

www.ingramcontent.com/pod-product-compliance
Lightning Source LLC
Chambersburg PA
CBHW030537210326
41597CB00014B/1192